ALBUM OF A NATION

ALBUM OF A NATION
THE MANY FACES OF BRITAIN

THE PRESS ASSOCIATION

PADDINGTON PRESS LTD
NEW YORK & LONDON

Frontispiece: Queen Victoria was born on May 24, 1819 and
succeeded to the throne on June 20, 1837. She died on
January 22, 1901 having reigned for more than sixty-three years.

Library of Congress Cataloging in Publication Data

Main entry under title:

Album of a nation.

1. Great Britain—Social life and customs—19th
century.   2. Great Britain—Social life and customs—
20th century.   3. Windsor, House of.   I. Press
Association, Ltd.
DA533.A54   941   79-10692

ISBN 0 448 22839 4 (U.S. and Canada only)
ISBN 0 7092 0627 5

Filmset in England by BAS Printers Limited,
Over Wallop, Hampshire
Printed and bound in England by Wm. Clowes & Sons Ltd.,
Beccles.
Designed by Colin Lewis

In the United States
PADDINGTON PRESS
Distributed by
GROSSET & DUNLAP

In the United Kingdom
PADDINGTON PRESS

In Canada
Distributed by
RANDOM HOUSE OF CANADA LTD.

In Southern Africa
Distributed by
ERNEST STANTON (PUBLISHERS) (PTY.) LTD.

In Australia and New Zealand
Distributed by
A. H. & A. W. REED

CONTENTS

INTRODUCTION

THE PICTURE LIBRARY of The Press Association, Britain's national news agency, contains a million and a half photographic prints going back over one hundred years. Together they make up a unique and valuable documentation of British life.

Newspapers can be an historical record and a nation's diary. Their news pictures can form its family album—a vivid witness of change and tradition. Six generations of the Royal Family, eccentricities of character and custom, sport and politics are captured by the news photographer who, often unwittingly, becomes an artist portraying the national life of his times.

Album of a Nation is our attempt to create a national family album—a pictorial record of a century of life in this country seen through the eyes of the professional news photographer.

The selections for this album represent untold hours of discussion and argument by three people who have totally different attitudes to photography. We are all senior executives of The Press Association, but there our common approach stops. Eric Pothecary, the picture editor, is a competitive news man whose yardstick is, not surprisingly, the news impact of any photograph we issue. Reg Eggleton, the commercial photos manager, promptly assesses the sales value of a print, and is concerned with all he sees in the frame, from light and shade to the finish a customer will require. My own involvement, as the agency's financial controller and company secretary, is different again.

I brought the three of us together to produce this book and with our differing viewpoints, we each struggled through boxes in the agency's archives which contained thousands of contact prints—to arrive at a more manageable selection for joint discussion. Our first choices amounted to nearly three thousand pictures; in a gradually winnowing process we got that total down to seven hundred and then down again to half as many. There were favourites, disagreements and no doubt injured feelings, but we ended up with the pictures you see on these pages.

So much for our differences. Where did we agree? The formula was a direct one. Our rule of thumb was to include any photograph which merited a second look . . . and a third, with the ultimate aim of producing a collection which would capture the essence of British life and character over the last century. Amongst the selection are personal favourites and national prize-winners. Some pictures are familiar and famous, remaining as captivating as they were on the day they first appeared in a morning edition. But many of them have never been seen by the public before— and we are delighted to present these unique discoveries.

Pictures, like copy, reach the news desk at all hours of

OPPOSITE: The man who took off his collar. Seaside holiday-makers on the beach at Bournemouth. 1946

6

the day or night. This fact is inescapable for those who work within the bustle of newspaper offices. It is a fact which also fits in well with the image of The Press Association—or PA as it is known within Britain's news industry—because it never closes its doors.

The Press Association was started in 1868 by enthusiastic Victorian newspaper publishers up and down the country, to assure themselves of a continuing and impeccable flow of news that would match any appearing in rival London dailies. Without a break, through war and peace, the PA has been doing that ever since, even though it now serves the metropolitan publishers and broadcasters as well.

One by one, former competitors in the news agency world dropped out or turned to specialization and the PA was left as the only national news agency; alone providing around the clock the great tide of news covering everything from Parliament to sport, from legal tussles to human disaster.

In volume alone the reporting service is remarkable. Over 200,000 words, enough for two major books, tumble from the teleprinter each day. The agency's banks of teleprinters do duty in the offices of the big London newspapers and the smaller dailies published far away, with the help of such refinements as long distance teletypesetting and the transmission of pictures over the wire.

Good pictures come in all the time, and we drew from them up to the last minute. Our choices may reflect a degree of personal preference, but we hope they will represent some of the many aspects which make up our national identity and will provoke memories for everyone.

It is impossible to acknowledge by name all those past and present members of the PA's photographic team without whose efforts over the years these photographs and this book would not have been possible. However, I must record my particular gratitude to Hilda Richards, Chief Picture Librarian, and the present darkroom staff for their ready assistance in sorting and processing the negatives of the selected photographs.

I am particularly grateful to Terry Timblick, PA Features Editor, and to Bill Martin, PA Chief Sports Reporter. Their enthusiasm and assistance in the caption writing and textual material is beyond praise.

My thanks also to Jack Auld, former External Relations Manager of the PA, for his ready and helpful advice and last but not least to my secretary, Eileen Sunderland, who has willingly undertaken all the secretarial work required in putting together a book of this nature.

Jack Purdham
THE PRESS ASSOCIATION

OPPOSITE: Rain stopped play at Worcester cricket ground. May 1967

THE ROYAL FAMILY

CORONATIONS, JUBILEES and State Tours are the familiar settings for the monarchy in Britain. On such occasions the Royal Family appears to bear the whole weight of history as they uphold traditions which have endured through successive reigns. Remote and majestic, they fulfil the roles of state in a way which has not changed very much over the last hundred years. The ritual and timelessness of these state functions only serve to emphasize their distance from ordinary life.

The pomp and circumstance is, however, balanced by a more human role and by a different type of continuity. A former Prince of Wales, later Edward VIII, was proud of being referred to as 'a good sport' and his willing participation in a wide range of sporting activities won admiration and affection. Today, Prince Charles, the current Prince of Wales, has been known to try everything from polo to parachuting. Almost every member of the Royal Family has been closely associated with a favourite sport.

But these photographs also bear witness to change. Years have seen the Royal Family brought closer to the people, and not just through a development in photographic technique. Informal 'walkabouts' characterize a new style of meeting the people. As ordinary people have increasingly moved into the picture, affection and understanding has deepened and a new role for the monarchy has been created. In the end, it is obvious that any collection of royal photographs reveals just as much about us as it does about them.

OPPOSITE: The Duke of Edinburgh pays homage to Queen Elizabeth II during the Coronation ceremony in Westminster Abbey. June 1953

The physical likeness between King George V and his cousin, Czar Nicholas of Russia, was always a theme of general comment. This picture, taken in 1913, proves the point. King George is on the right.

King George V (right) and his cousin Kaiser Wilhelm II leave the Potsdam Palace to attend the annual review of the Potsdam garrison. May 1913

Princess May of Teck in her 'coming out' gown, 1884. The princess married George, second son of King Edward VII on July 6, 1893. George succeeded to the throne in 1910, as George V—Princess May became Queen Mary.

Queen Mary in the dress she wore for the State Opening of Parliament, February 2, 1926.

TOP: King George V reviews his troops! The orderly ranks are the children of men of the Tank Corps stationed at Lulworth, Dorset. 1928. BOTTOM: King George V, an excellent shot, in his shooting suit of light brown tweeds, Homburg hat, boots and shooting spats at Sandringham, the country home of the Royal Family. January 26, 1928

TOP: The King, this time in Naval uniform receives admiring glances from the women workers when he visits the works of the Clyde Shipbuilding and Engineering Company, Glasgow. September 1917 BOTTOM: Prince John, seen here in 1917 under the critical eye of his father, King George V. A delicate child from birth he died in 1919 at the age of thirteen.

King George V on tour of the Manchester area in 1917 uses the workmen's time clock at the Westinghouse Works, Trafford Park.

The Prince and Princess of Wales, later to become King George V and Queen Mary, suitably dressed for a visit to Liskeard, Cornwall to open a new shaft in the Phoenix Tin Mine. 1908

British monarchs held the title of Emperor of India from 1877 to 1947. In 1911 King George V and Queen Mary visited India. The high point of the tour was the Coronation Durbar in Delhi.

The Royal couple are shown leaving the dais after the reading of the Proclamation of the King's Coronation at Westminster (above) and (right) appearing on a balcony at a later function.

King George V, centre in carriage, arriving at the Epsom races, 1911, to thc obvious delight of the gypsy children running alongside.

Mr. Woodrow Wilson, President of the United States, with his wife (extreme left) photographed with King George V, Queen Mary and their daughter Princess Mary outside Buckingham Palace during his visit to London in 1918.

Queen Mary, visiting the Rachel McMillan Memorial
Training College at Deptford, London, with some of the
children from the nursery school attached to the college.
May 1930

One hundred and eleven servicemen were listed dead or missing from Palace Road, Hackney, London, during the first two years of the 1914–18 war. Queen Mary inspects the Roll of Honour. 1916

Queen Mary, visiting the International Wool Exhibition in London, examines a white wool evening dress designed by Paquin of France. September 21, 1949

OPPOSITE: Queen Mary and Queen Alexandra chat with bridesmaids after the wedding of Lord Louis Mountbatten. July 1922

King George V talks to a young dockyard worker during a 1918 visit to a Sunderland shipyard.

21

King George V (centre) and Queen Mary on
his left on board the P & O vessel *Medina*,
manned for the occasion by the Royal Navy.
The King and Queen were en route for India.
1911

23

The Prince of Wales, later King Edward VIII, a second lieutenant in the Grenadier Guards, marching with his regiment. 1914

The Braemar Gathering, in September 1921, the setting for the Highland Games, sees the Prince in a kilt.

On board *HMS Renown* at the end of a short visit to Japan, May 1922. The Prince is wearing the dress of a Japanese coolie.

The Prince dressed in his uniform as Colonel-in-Chief of the 35th and 36th Jacob's Horse in Delhi, India. February 1922

The Prince of Wales was a welcome visitor to this miner's
home during his tour of the mining districts of northern
England. Middleston Moor, County Durham, February
1929

The Prince of Wales in Weymouth to open the harbour and pier. July 13, 1933

The Prince leaves the Cymncr pithead, Wales, after a visit below ground. June 1919

Convalescing from measles, the young Prince Edward, always a keen sportsman, finds time for a game of golf in Newquay, March 1911. Later in the year he was formally invested in Caernarvon Castle with the title, Prince of Wales.

The Prince of Wales, not exactly dressed for the occasion, starts an exhibition soccer match between Fulham FC and Tottenham Hotspur FC at Sandhurst Military College. May 14, 1921

The Prince of Wales, in Malta for the opening of
Parliament, taking part in a sack race at a local gymkhana
and (right) competing with his cousin, Lord Louis
Mountbatten, in the 'King's Messenger' race. November
8, 1921

The Duchess of York receives a farewell embrace from the Prince of Wales aboard *HMS Renown* before the Duke and Duchess departed for their tour of New Zealand and Australia in 1927.

A Royal 'rule' was broken at Epsom on Derby Day, June 1928, when the Prince went into the paddock.

The Prince of Wales and the Begum of Bhopal on their way
to the Durbar Hall at Sadar Manzil Palace. February 1922

OPPOSITE: The Duke and Duchess of York on honeymoon at Polesden Lacey in Surrey, May 1, 1923. The house was made available to the Royal couple by the Hon. Mrs. Ronald Greville.

Military drill under the eagle eye of a Sergeant Major of the Coldstream Guards was considered essential training for the young Princes, Henry (left) and George. 1909

The Prince of Wales (left), a keen and daring rider in steeplechase events, with the Duke of York and Prince Henry at the Army point-to-point races, Arborfield Cross, March 1924. Prince Henry and the Prince of Wales were competitors.

King George V (left) riding in Windsor Great Park, March 1923, with his four sons. Left to right are Edward, Prince of Wales, later King Edward VIII and following his abdication in December 1936, Duke of Windsor; Albert, Duke of York, who following Edward's abdication became King George VI; Prince Henry, later the Duke of Gloucester; and, on the extreme right, Prince George, later the Duke of Kent, who was killed in a flying accident while serving with the Royal Air Force during the Second World War.

King George V at the wheel of his yacht
Britannia. 1924

King George V, nearing the end of his
Coronation Durbar visit to India, lunches in
the jungle at Nepal. The King (first left) was
in Nepal to enjoy ten days' big-game shooting.
December 1912

The christening of Princess Elizabeth, a future Queen, in
May 1926. The princess wore the cream Brussels lace robe
worn on similar occasions by her Royal grandparents and
great-grandparents. The sponsors were the Duke of Con-
naught (extreme left), Princess Mary (extreme right), the
grandparents, King George V and Queen Mary, and the
Earl and Countess of Strathmore.

The Duke of Duchess of York with their daughter Princess Elizabeth. May 1926

This visit to a function of the 'Lest We Forget Association' at the Molesley and Hampton Court Branch in 1924 is typical of the personal interest shown by The Duchess of York in many social activities and charitable organizations.

When Duchess of York, the Queen Mother's warm and cheerful personality was an obviously welcome tonic to staff and invalids at the British Home and Hospital for Incurables, Putney, visited in 1928.

The Duchess of York attends the London Exhibition of embroideries produced by disabled ex-servicemen. The young Princess Elizabeth takes a welcome rest in her personal chair used for these occasions. 1929

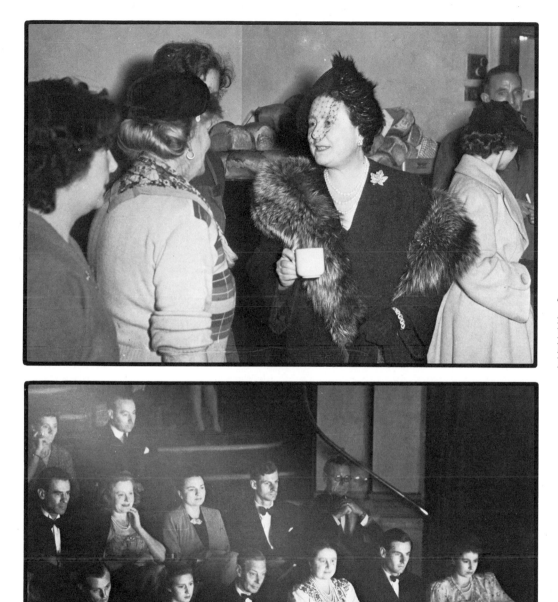

The Queen Mother talks to some of those made homeless by the floods in the Thames Estuary. Princess Margaret who accompanied her mother is to the right of the picture. February 1953

King George VI and Queen Elizabeth with Princess Elizabeth (right) and Princess Margaret watching a performance at the Strand Theatre, London. Seated second right is Group Capt. Peter Townsend. August 1946

The regal figure of Queen Elizabeth the
Queen Mother attending the Commonwealth
concert held in St. James's Palace, London, to
celebrate the golden jubilee in 1960 of the
Royal Over-Seas League.

In the spring of 1969 the Queen Mother enjoys an early hothouse-grown strawberry at the Chelsea Flower Show, held in the grounds of the Royal Hospital in London.

43

The young Princesses Elizabeth (left) and Margaret Rose 'ride out' with their Nanny, Nurse Clara Knight or 'Alla' as she was affectionately known to her charges. March 22, 1933

Princess Elizabeth (left) and Princess Margaret riding on Bonza Beach, South Africa. March 12, 1947

44

Another generation and another Royal christening. Princess Elizabeth holds Prince Charles, her son and a future direct heir to the throne, at Buckingham Palace, December 15, 1948. The christening robe was that worn by the Princess at her christening.

Princess Elizabeth and Prince Philip on their wedding day, November 20, 1947, wave to the crowd from the balcony of Buckingham Palace.

A backward glance from Princess Anne, as with her husband, Captain Mark Phillips, she leaves Westminster Abbey after their wedding. November 14, 1973

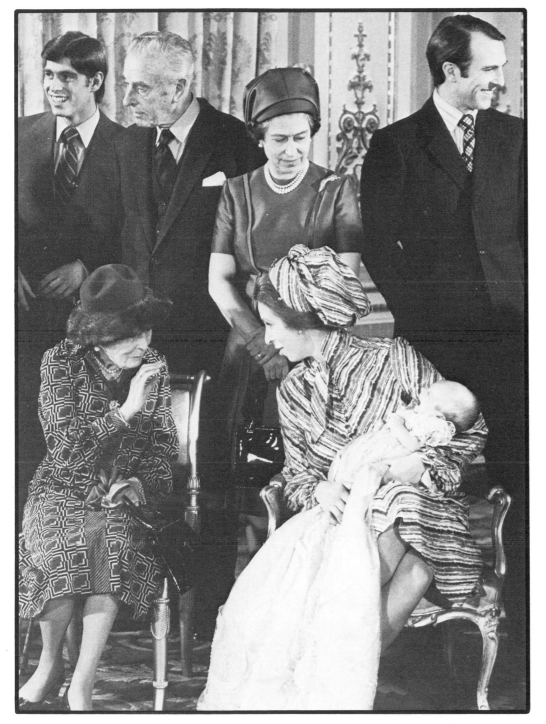

Some advice for the young mother, Princess Anne, from Princess Alice, Countess of Athlone, granddaughter of Queen Victoria, and the great-great-great aunt of baby Peter Mark Andrew who had earlier been christened in the Music Room of Buckingham Palace by the Archbishop of Canterbury. (Back row: left to right) Prince Andrew, Earl Mountbatten of Burma, The Queen, and Captain Mark Phillips. December 22, 1977

A charming picture of The Queen, when Princess Elizabeth, wearing a tiara and carrying a huge bouquet of flowers when attending the Premiere at a London theatre of the British film *The Lady with a Lamp*, first screened in 1951.

The Queen, on a Metropolitan Police horse, a grey named Doctor, taking the salute as the Guards march past outside Buckingham Palace after the Trooping the Colour ceremony in June 1966.

No modern Sir Walter Raleigh gallantry was offered on this perfect opportunity, but The Queen holding her umbrella, cheerfully faced the prospect of wet feet and continued a walkabout in Blenheim during her Silver Jubilee tour of New Zealand. 1977

A big smile from The Queen when she presented new Colours to the First Battalion of the Irish Guards at Windsor Castle in May 1978. Her hat, decorated with butterflies, and her coat were in St. Patrick's blue to match the plumes of the Guards' Bearskins.

An historic scene—photographed and tele-
vised for the first time—the State Opening
of Parliament. The Queen, wearing the
Imperial Crown, is seated on the throne with
the Duke of Edinburgh seated to her left.
Viscount Montgomery, holding the Sword of
State, stands to the left front of the Duke.
The Earl of Home with the Cap of
Maintenance stands on the other side of the
dais. House of Lords, Westminster, London.
October 28, 1958

The investiture of new Knights Companions of the Order of the Garter is a colourful ceremony which takes place in Windsor Castle. The year 1348 is accepted as the date of institution of this ancient Order.

51

The Duke and Duchess of Windsor watching the Coronation of Queen Elizabeth II on television at the Paris home of a friend. June 3, 1953

Royal fashion at Royal Ascot and a delighted owner, The Queen, waits for her winning horse, Alexander, to return to the paddock after winning the Royal Hunt Cup. With the Queen are her trainer, Captain Cecil Boyd-Rochfort and (left to right) Princess Margaret, the Queen Mother, the Princess Royal, the Duchess of Kent, and (extreme right) the Duchess of Gloucester. June 26, 1956

The wedding of Princess Anne and Captain Mark Phillips at Westminster Abbey, November 14, 1973. The Queen and the Queen Mother watch the couple leave the Abbey after the ceremony. The bridegroom's parents are behind the Royal party.

The Queen enjoys a joke at St. Katherine Dock, on a 'meet the people' walk during the Silver Jubilee river trip from Greenwich to Lambeth. June 9, 1977

Two-year-old Tracy Selby did not wait for a Royal 'thank you' after presenting The Queen with roses. The Queen was visiting Carmarthen on the second day of her Silver Jubilee tour of Wales. June 23, 1977

The Queen receives some camera hints from Lord Mountbatten
at the Royal Windsor Horse Show. May 1973

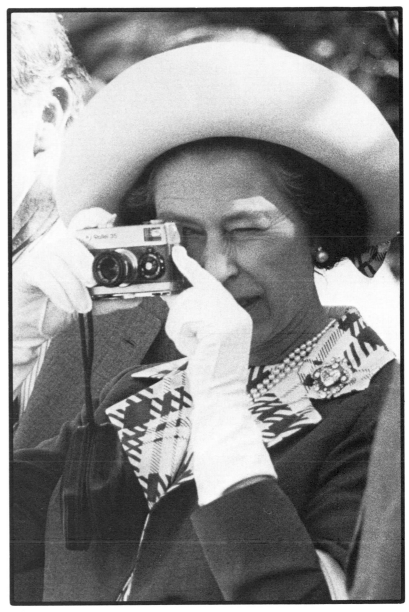

The Queen records a personal memory of her visit to
Lindsay Park Stud, South Australia. March 1977

The Queen, at Badminton with other members of the Royal
Family for the Horse Trials, finds one of the events out of
sight but not out of the range of the TV camera. April 1973

The Queen takes a close look at the crowded banks of
instruments on the flight deck of Concorde during her flight
home from Bridgetown, Barbados, after her Silver Jubilee
tour of the West Indies. November 2, 1977

After returning from his Christmas holiday of 1957 at Sandringham, Prince Charles, carrying his case and coat with cap pulled well down, went unnoticed through the ticket barrier at Newbury Station on his way to start the new term at Cheam School.

The Prince of Wales precedes The Queen
through the Nave of Westminster Abbey after
the ceremony where the Prince was installed
as Great Master of the Most Honourable
Order of the Bath. This occasion, in 1975,
was the 250th anniversary service of the
Order.

59

Princess Anne, riding Goodwill in the cross-country
section of the Army Horse Trials at Tidworth, May 1975.
The Princess is a keen competitor and has represented
Britain in international events.

The first competitive polo game for Prince Charles, the
Combermere Cup competition in Windsor Great Park,
April 23, 1967. The Prince, left of picture, scored a goal.
His father, the Duke of Edinburgh, is in the centre.

A keen sportsman, the Duke of Edinburgh is
seen bowling for the local cricket team of
Mersham-le-Hatch against the neighbouring
village of Aldington. The record shows that
the Duke took three wickets for twenty-seven
runs and the Mersham team won the match.
Princess Elizabeth and the Duke of Edinburgh
were spending the weekend in Mersham
at the home of Lord and Lady Brabourne.

July 31, 1949

Prince Charles is not unwilling to try most sports. His attempt at wind-surfing in the Solent during Cowes week in August 1978 was not without mishap but practice makes perfect.

The Queen and Prince Edward, her youngest son, shield their ears from the aircraft noise during the 'fly past' at the Silver Jubilee Review of RAF Finningley. July 29, 1977

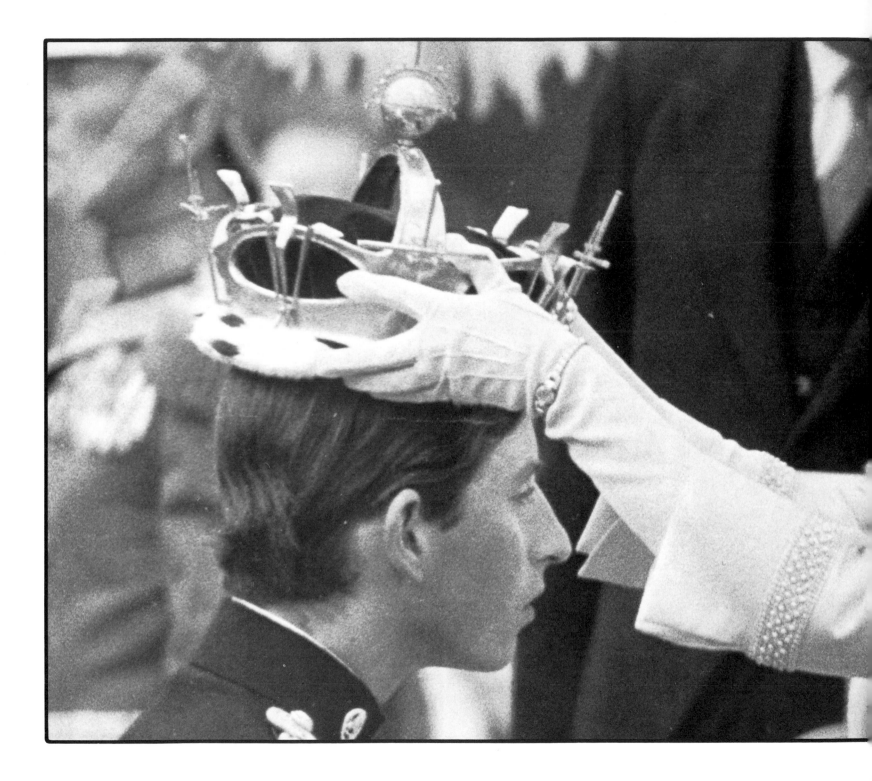

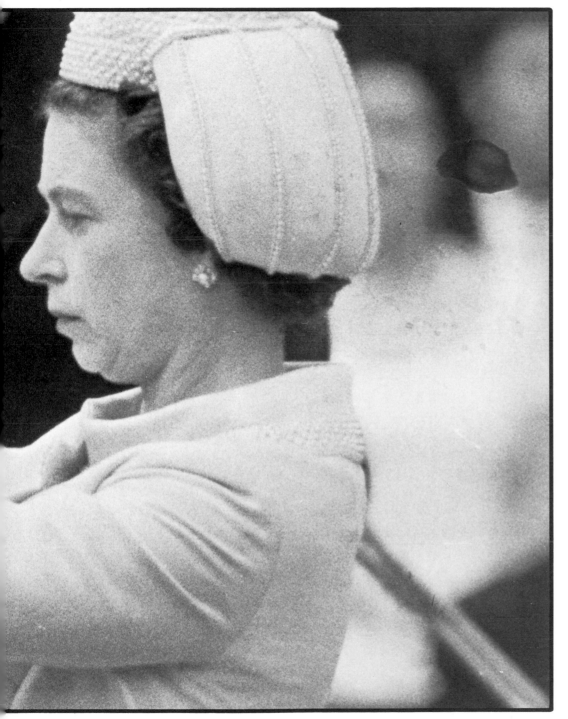

The Investiture of the Prince of Wales at
Caernarvon Castle on July 1, 1969. The
Queen places the coronet on the head of the
young prince.

67

POLITICS AND PERSONALITIES

A QUARTER-MILE of London pavement, and a busy crossing, is the walking distance from the Houses of Parliament to the Prime Minister's residence in Downing Street—the famous Number Ten. But to complete that journey politically—to make the epic jump from MP to Premier—may require more than direction, survival or the ambition to stride proprietorially across the most illustrious threshold in British public life.

Sheer style can often seem to be the decisive factor. It is a quality which in this century alone has been colourfully varied, expressed in the cut of a raincoat, the jut of a pipe or cigar, the obstinacy of an eyebrow.

Looks, not laws, are what many occupants of Downing Street are best remembered for. Style seems to convey reassurance and continuity, even if the past is not unblemished by crisis. The politics of avuncularism is nothing new.

Other figures in the public eye do not have Downing Street as their ultimate destination. They may be aspiring to the stage, screen or the summit of Everest, but the same photogenic qualities can often be used to even greater effect.

If this gallery of famous faces unconsciously fashioned their 'images' before such preoccupations were common, nevertheless they arrived at a kind of visual shorthand which in time becomes indivisible from the way they are affectionately remembered.

OPPOSITE.: Rhetoric in the making. Winston Churchill and his secretary at home in Sussex Square, London, working on the 1924 Abbey by-election campaign. As an Independent anti-Socialist, he lost by forty-three votes, but six months later he was an MP again, and in the Cabinet.

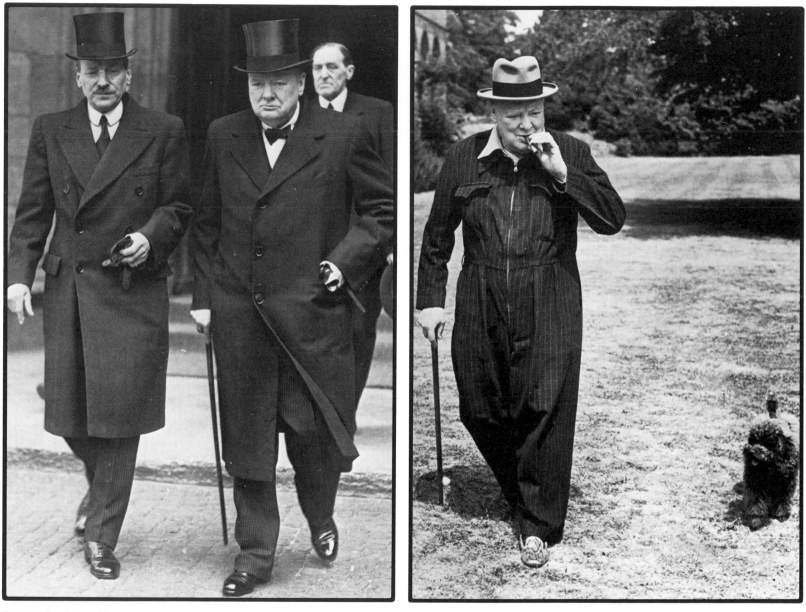

Grief's 'uniform' hid political differences for Premier Attlee and wartime coalition government leader Churchill at a 1946 memorial service.

Even four years after the wailings of air raid sirens ceased, Churchill's famous wartime siren suit was still in vogue with its owner, at his country home, Chartwell, Kent.

Before or since, it's hard to name any other Chancellor of the Exchequer playing polo at the age of fifty. Churchill helped the Commons beat the Lords at Ranelagh in 1925.

The Prince of Wales, later Edward VIII, with Churchill after a Commons lunch to honour two U.S. fliers who had 'hopped' the Atlantic in a Curtiss seaplane. 1919

1913—the year of the multi-layered camper. David Lloyd George, who became Prime Minister in 1916, and his wife stoically sampling the outdoor life at the base of Moel Heboz, North Wales.

Fashionably dressed, but looking rather grim, Prime Minister Asquith and his wife leave St. Paul's Cathedral, 1916.

Economic outlook dull, but becoming brighter? Presenting
a Budget is a serious business or so Chancellor of the
Exchequer Neville Chamberlain suggests, setting out for
the House of Commons in 1933.

R. A. Butler makes a graceful arrival at 10 Downing Street,
for a Cabinet meeting in 1955. As Chancellor of the Exchequer, he
was bearing tidings of International Monetary Fund
deliberations in Istanbul.

Among young candidates at a pre-General Election Tory Party briefing session in 1951 was Margaret Roberts (24), who in 1975, as Mrs. Thatcher, became the first woman Party Leader. With her is Lord Woolton, Conservative chairman 1946–55.

'What big eyebrows you have, Grandpa.' The Chancellor of the Exchequer, Denis Healey, looks a little rattled by six-month-old Thomas Copsey. Mrs. Healey enjoys the eye-level exchanges. April 1976

Defence Secretary Fred Mulley, possibly the victim of a low cloud, at the Silver Jubilee Review of the Royal Air Force in July 1977 — at RAF Finningley near Doncaster. The gaze of The Queen and Prince Philip was dutifully on target.

To Russia with love. Premier Harold Wilson saying goodbye to his wife Mary at Downing Street, January 1968, prior to his three-day visit to Moscow.

Ex-Prime Minister Edward Heath still calling
the tune—rehearsing the European Community Youth Orchestra for their summer
tour in 1978.

Edwardian women with a cause. Suffragette leader Mrs.
Emmeline Pankhurst, second right, with her daughter
Christabel (right) and other early figures in the movement.
1908

'I am a Virginian, so naturally I am a politician,' declared Lady Nancy Astor, who in 1919, for Plymouth, became the first woman Member of Parliament. She is seated in the middle of this 1924 group on the Commons Terrace, with all but one of the other women MPs of the day. Female representation in the House did not continue at this pace. By July 1978, for example, of 635 MPs, only 27 were women.

As protocol decrees, the Gentleman Usher of the Black Rod approaches the Speaker (wearing a full wig) and summons the Members of the House of Commons to the Bar of the House of Lords for the State Opening of Parliament in 1974.

Flanked by colleagues, Premier James Callaghan waits
reflectively in the House of Commons for the summons to
the House of Lords for the State Opening of Parliament in
1976.

Ready for an intellectual heavyweight bout are George
Bernard Shaw and G. K. Chesterton, flanking Hilaire
Belloc who 'refereed' their debate in 1927 on the topic 'Do
we agree?'

From
Bernard Shaw

Phone & Wire:
CODICOTE 218.

AYOT SAINT LAWRENCE.
WELWYN, HERTS.

15/6/1947

I know nothing new nor
interesting about India or Egypt.
How can I or anyone tell what
will happen in the next 10 or
15 years. I cannot tell what
will happen tomorrow.

I positively will not write
about India. It is not my
subject.

G. B. S.

Postcard brevity from GBS.

Two years wiser, or curiouser, GBS displays an interest in India by receiving Premier Pandit Nehru at Ayot St. Lawrence, Shaw's home in Hertfordshire.

Star of her own show, revue artiste Beatrice
Lillie marries Robert Peel in 1920.

Fashionable holiday pose by Beatrice Lillie at Cap d'Antibes, French Riviera, 1932.

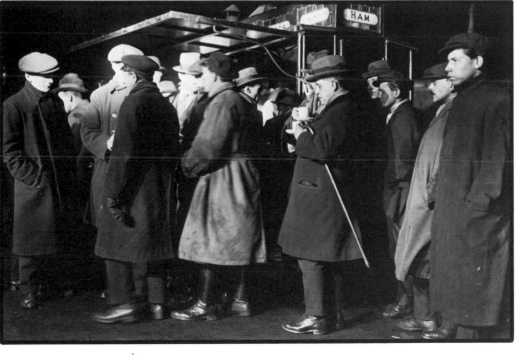

Among the 1.30 A.M. patrons of a Charing Cross coffee stall in December 1921, was playwright James Barrie (with stick), author of *Peter Pan*.

Off to America. Noël Coward at Waterloo station in 1925 with leading lady Lillian Braithwaite.

Sounding musical at the age of thirteen. Julie Andrews rehearses for the 1948 Royal Variety Performance at the London Palladium.

Charlie Chaplin in 1919 (the year he formed United Artists with Douglas Fairbanks, Mary Pickford and D. W. Griffith). His companion is *Sphere* magazine's London editor, Clement Shorter.

Kate Carney, music hall artiste, in Cockney coster suit of 'pearlies'. 1917

The actress whose most famous role was off stage, as mistress of Edward VII, Lillie Langtry (then Lady de Bathe) at her Newmarket home. 1919

Theatrical luminaries of 1928—Ivor Novello and Lily Elsie.

Lady Diana Duff Cooper, a well-known beauty and socialite, and her husband arrive for a charity film in 1922.

Moment of high drama for Diana Duff Cooper as the Madonna in *The Miracle*, a 1932 stage production.

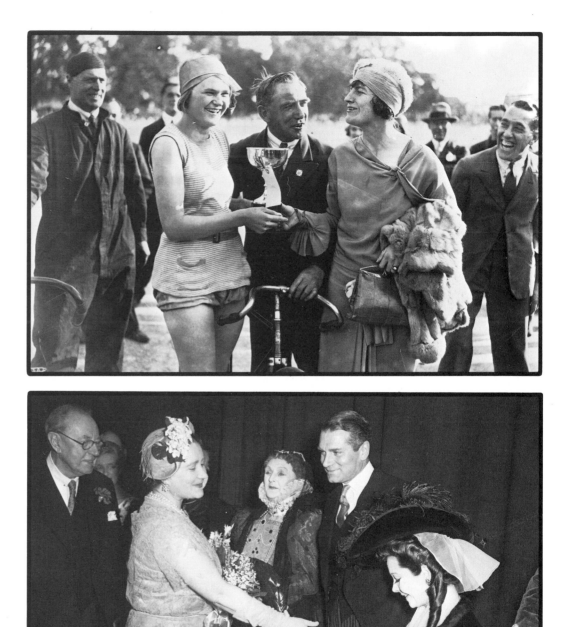

Singer Gracie Fields rewards a cycling
champion at London's Herne Hill. 1929

Queen Elizabeth the Queen Mother in 1954
with stars of the English stage: Vivien Leigh,
curtseying, Laurence Olivier and Sybil
Thorndike.

An investiture out of doors by a reigning monarch is a rare occasion. Dubbed knight aboard *HMS Princess Royal* in 1916 is Admiral W. C. Pakenham, honoured by George V.

Monarch and men. George V with his own Company of
Grenadier Guards at Windsor Castle. 1926

One of Britain's greatest spies. Wing-Commander F. F. E. Yeo-Thomas, whose wartime exploits won him fame and the alias 'The White Rabbit', tries on a new hat on de-mobilisation in 1946.

Models were still known as mannequins in 1950. Barbara Goalen in typically stylish pose.

Mrs. Gertrude Shilling, queen of overstatement at Royal Ascot every year, embellishing 1974 with mink and fox fur finery.

Fashion designer Mary Quant, aptly garbed, en route to judge a 1966 mini-skirt contest.

Twiggy and her manager Justin de Villeneuve leave for an export-boosting trip to Denmark in 1968.

Inventor John Logie Baird with his television apparatus at the Science Museum in 1926.

On trial for murdering his wife: the infamous Dr. Crippen and Ethel Le Neve at the Old Bailey in 1910. He was found guilty and hanged; she was acquitted.

Off duty at Lord's cricket ground, 1913.
Scout movement founder, Sir Robert Baden-
Powell, and his wife.

His camel-power days behind him, 'Lawrence
of Arabia' as the anonymous T. E. Shaw in
the RAF. 1927

97

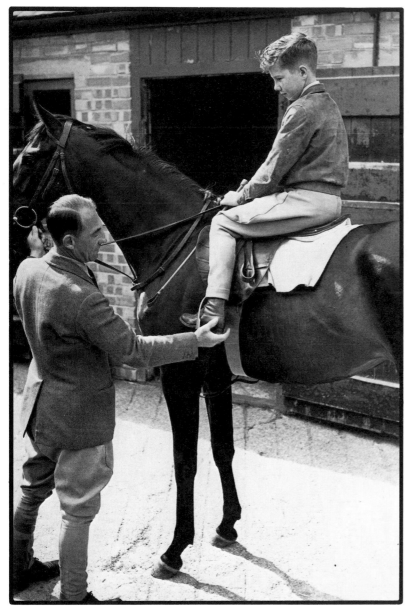

Lester Piggott, aged twelve in 1948, youngest British jockey to win a race, with his father Keith, a former steeplechaser. Grandfather Ernie Piggott won the Grand National three times.

Lester Piggott beams with pleasure after winning the Derby for the eighth time—a racing record. June 1977

The first Everest conquerors, Edmund Hillary and Sherpa
Tensing with Colonel John Hunt (centre) at Katmandu,
Nepal after the British expedition's successful ascent of the
mountain in May 1953.

THE SPORTING SPIRIT

BRITAIN BOASTS A fascinating variety of sporting activities, many of which owe their origin to native inventiveness. If a few of these national pastimes are not fully understood the world over, each provides special drama and a chance to demonstrate unique skills.

Apart from the weather, sport is probably one of the greatest topics of conversation in Britain. The average sports enthusiast may be an armchair expert, but expert he certainly is. From the terraces at Wembley at an international football match to the pavilion at Lord's where England meet the old enemy, Australia, at cricket, advice and opinion is given freely and without encouragement. Not surprisingly, a strong sense of gamesmanship and fair play is deeply rooted in the British personality, although such tolerance may be noticeably absent if you dare to criticize someone's football team!

A host of traditional events dominate the sporting year. High summer brings the Derby at Epsom, a Test match at Lord's, Henley Regatta and Wimbledon fortnight—all within a few weeks of each other. These occasions offer the spectator a chance to see all the extremes of competitive emotion—despair, hilarity, triumph and exhilaration.

The photograph gives privileged access to spectacular moments in sporting history and immortalizes the great heroes of the past, from the legendary cricketer W. G. Grace to the first man to run a four minute mile, Roger Bannister.

OPPOSITE: They didn't call football matches off for a shower of rain in those days! Not surprisingly, this picture of the former England and Preston winger, Tom Finney, losing himself in a cloud of spray, at Chelsea in 1956, won first prize as the outstanding sports picture of that year.

Alex Forbes, Arsenal's Scottish international half-back, arriving in a hurry as the legendary Stanley Matthews shapes to centre the ball in a match between Arsenal and Blackpool in 1952. Matthews played in the First Division at the age of fifty.

Chelsea goalkeeper, Peter Bonetti, known as 'The Cat' because of his remarkable agility, gets airborne to turn a Liverpool shot round the post in the F.A. Cup semi-final in 1965.

. . . and Gordon West of Blackpool, having apparently made an unsuccessful attempt to catch the ball in his mouth, ties himself into a knot to make an equally spectacular save. 1961   103

OPPOSITE: All eyes are on Gareth Edwards, the Welsh Rugby number nine, as France mount an attack at Cardiff (1976). Edwards retired two years later after setting a Welsh record of fifty-three caps.

Graham Joyce, Bradford Northern's second row forward, is comprehensively tackled by Featherstone's Alan Rhodes and Jim Thompson in the Rugby League Cup final at Wembley. 1973

Never mind the ball, let's get on with the game! The England trial at Taunton in 1958 presented the selectors with all sorts of problems. For instance, the player second from the right is actually wearing a white shirt.

OPPOSITE: Penny farthings in action at Herne Hill. Punctures were no problem. 1932

On the right, Reg Harris on the way to completing one of the most remarkable comebacks in British sport. Harris, top cycle sprinter just after the war is seen beating British champion, Reg Barnett in 1971—at the age of fifty-one.

All the grace and elegance of a top jumping horse, and plenty of concentration from his rider, Alan Oliver, as Red Admiral takes a fence at the International Show at White City. July, 1954

In the grounds of Arundel Castle, Pat Smythe, then world's leading lady rider, puts Flanagan over the water, in training for the 1960 Olympic Games.

Sometimes the horse makes the decision as Derek Kent discovered at the Royal Windsor Horse Show. 1954

OPPOSITE: The grounds of Castle Combe
Manor, Wiltshire, provide a pastoral setting
for a meeting of the Beaufort Hunt. The
Duke of Beaufort faces the camera.
November 1948

Red Rum's record third victory in the Grand
National in 1977, brings a risky response from
his supporters near the finishing line at
Aintree.

A big field at full gallop as they round the
bend at Royal Ascot. June 1953

110

Archery, a sedate sport requiring great concentration, is practised by women at a meeting in London in 1908.

Lacrosse produces a flying ballet of movement. England
meet the United States. London, 1951

Messrs. Ross, in the white breeches, and Collinson, with
the cauliflower ear, square up with bare knuckles in 1914.

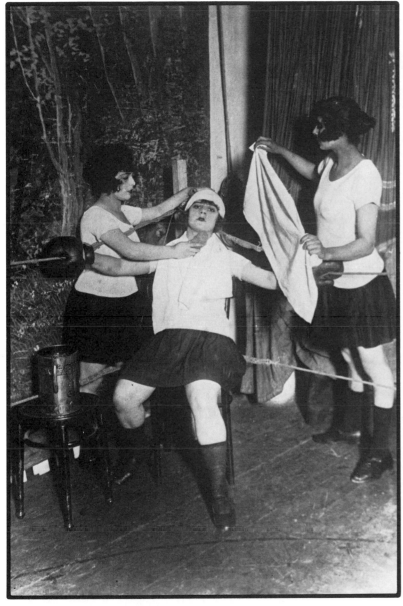

Miss X receives attention from her seconds between rounds, in a ladies' boxing tournament. 1921

Cassius Clay (Muhammad Ali) hits the floor. Henry Cooper, who has just connected with a left hook, surveys the result of his handiwork. But Clay got up to win. June 1963

OPPOSITE: An historic moment at Iffley Road, Oxford, on a cold evening in May 1954. Roger Bannister becomes the first man to run a mile inside four minutes. Running for the AAA against his former university, he clocks 3 minutes 59.14 seconds.

Dorando Pietri of Italy heroically won the 1908 Olympic marathon in London but was disqualified for being assisted near the finish. Four times he was picked up by officials after collapsing, at the end of the 26 mile 385 yard race.

Full stretch for the line as England's Sonia Lannaman (number three) and Andrea Lynch (number six) show Canada and Poland the way home in an international at Crystal Palace.

OPPOSITE: Near the start of the Olympic marathon in 1908, the Canadians, with cyclists in attendance, trot through Windsor on the way to London.

Modest white bloomers were necessary equipment for the women's high jump in the 1908 Olympic Games, at White City, London. The competition does not look too exacting as the girls warm up.

David Hemery (right), who later became Olympic champion, shows the way as he wins the 400 metres hurdles for Oxford against Cambridge. His team mate, Christopher Brownlees (number three) was less elegant but still finished second. May 1970

Another fashion plate from athletics history. The well bandaged Mlle. Rillac of France and Miss Hatt of England at an international match in London, 1921.

Jeff Gutteridge goes on to clear 15 feet
7 inches at Crystal Palace. August 1975

Edward Heath, the former Prime Minister, appears to be the only one doing any work as he helms his yacht, *Morning Cloud*, during Cowes Week in 1978.

Perfect conditions at Cowes as the sails fill. The racing is close for the New York Yacht Club challenge cup. August 1978

Flying crewman Julian Roderick goes for a
ride on the spinnaker of *Whirlwind IV*, at
Cowes. August, 1977

The legendary Dr. W. G. Grace of Gloucestershire and England, probably England's best known cricketer, captained England against Australia in 1891–2 and is still remembered for performances back in the nineteenth century.

A risky bit of hurdling as a streaker introduces a new dimension to cricket at the Lord's Test between England and Australia. August 1975

Wasim Bari, the Pakistan wicket keeper, cannot decide whether to catch it or swallow it. In the end he caught it, and Mike Brearley of Middlesex, later Captain of England, departed for thirty-two runs. Lord's, 1974

There is no escape from a situation like this. A beautiful piece of bowling by Wayne Daniel of Middlesex and Leicestershire's Barry Dudleston is on his way. Lord's, 1978

. . . or this. The bails are still in the air as
Peter Denning of Somerset turns to survey
the wreckage in the Gillette Cup final against
Sussex. Lord's, 1978

The sartorial style matches the period as Ted Ray, one of the great golfers of his time, drives off from the eleventh tee at Deal. 1910

Ken Brown's chip missed by an inch in the 1977 Ryder Cup match, and how he suffers.

Stern, self-possessed and dressed in the height of golfing fashion, the Countess of Wilton plays at the Ladies Parliamentary meeting, Edgware, 1920.

Bobby Jones, the legendary American golfer, drives off at Sunningdale, 1926.

TOP: A 1922 Bentley with the Hon. G. A. Egerton at the wheel. BOTTOM: Even as recently as 1949, Grand Prix cars had a long way to go to catch up with the style of the modern Formula One cars. The start of the British Grand Prix at Silverstone.

TOP: A slightly more modern example of the racing car manufacturers' art, flat out on the banking at Brooklands. 1932. BOTTOM: Britain's James Hunt overtakes the reigning world champion, Niki Lauda, in the British Grand Prix, at Brands Hatch. 1976

The start of a two hundred mile race at Brooklands. The predicament of number fourteen explains why drivers carried mechanics. September 1925

Mlle. Lenglen, the famous Suzanne, with her partner, René Lacoste, the French Davis Cup player, on a collision course, in an exhibition at Roehampton. 1925

Helen Wills, a picture of 1924 modesty, beats Kitty McKane in the women's singles final at Wimbledon.

The same singles final, a quarter of a century later. Louise Brough defends her title against her American teammate, Margaret Du Pont. July 1949

Bjorn Borg, the young Swede who seems to have taken over the Centre Court at Wimbledon, gets tremendous weight into this shot against Arthur Ashe in 1975. Borg won the men's singles in 1978 for the third successive year.

Life is not always smooth for the man in the umpire's chair. Ilie Nastase of Rumania was in good verbal form during this 1977 men's singles at Wimbledon, against Andrew Pattison.

The moment that British tennis supporters have been able
to enjoy only three times since the war. Virginia Wade
holds the gold trophy aloft after winning the Wimbledon's
women's singles in 1977.

LIFE AND LEISURE

THE PEACEFUL COEXISTENCE of the predictable and the unexpected characterizes British life.

The British calendar is a garden of perennial events. In towns and villages, the nation's countless local customs enjoy annual airings, a medieval spirit of community disarming modern sophistication. Ancient usage gives respectability and dignity (or so onlookers and participants believe) to otherwise preposterous bits of revelry and ceremony—all in the happily innocuous homage to the past.

The quaint tyranny of the annual rituals which make up the English 'season' also forges links with the past. The grand occasions of Ascot and the Royal garden parties are social fixtures for the few, but enjoyed by many as part of the passing spectacle.

In pursuit of relaxation, the island holiday-maker is often at home by the sea. The phrase 'a day at the seaside' evokes a special kind of nostalgia for those accustomed to taking day trips to Blackpool, Bournemouth or Brighton.

Yet perhaps in response to the orderliness of such traditions, Britain has nurtured a conspicuously high density of oddness per square foot. The unexpected can happen anywhere, any time: in the whimsical world of fashion or in the domestic deification of assorted animals. These independent attitudes inevitably make for a mood of surprise.

OPPOSITE: An English garden party in the garden of 10, Downing Street, traditional home and office of the Prime Minister. The occasion was a fund raising event for the King George's Fund for Sailors. Mr. Clement Attlee, then the Prime Minister, is standing to the right of the picture. July 15, 1947

Royal Ascot has long been regarded as the fashion parade of the London season. Dressed in the latest fashion for the period are these ladies at the 1910 and 1914 summer race meetings.

Royal Ascot in 1936 (left) and 1939. Men's dress shows
little change.

Lady Alexandra Cavendish-Bentinck dressed for an afternoon 'drive'. June 1923

Mrs. Irene Castle, dance star of the pre-1914 era, who with her husband, Vernon, was considered to have established the popularity of modern ballroom dancing. Mrs. Castle was reported to be one of the world's best dressed women. December 1923

Oxford bags—the latest in trousers for the young man about town in the 1920s.

Lancashire coal miners in May 1946. Not fashionable dress but made to last!

'Exciting platform scenes', but not for this would-be
traveller reading a 'station closed' notice outside Snow Hill
railway station in London during a coal strike in 1912.

The rally call was for a mass meeting of dockers in Trafalgar
Square, December 1945, but a young boy appears the most
interested in the words of the speaker.

A keeper of the peace. A Royal Defence Force
sentry on duty outside Somerset House,
London, during a strike crisis in April 1921.

The 'Equal pay for Women' campaign advertised in the Strand, London, in 1952. The placard bearers, marching to Piccadilly Circus, included many professional women, some wishing to remain unidentified.

OPPOSITE: A variety of students' fashion 'modelled' by the picket line outside the London School of Economics. December 1971

In 1966 the cry was 'keep the mini-skirt' and members of 'The British Society for the Advancement of the Mini Skirt' protested outside Christian Dior's London premises during the showing of the Autumn/Winter collection.

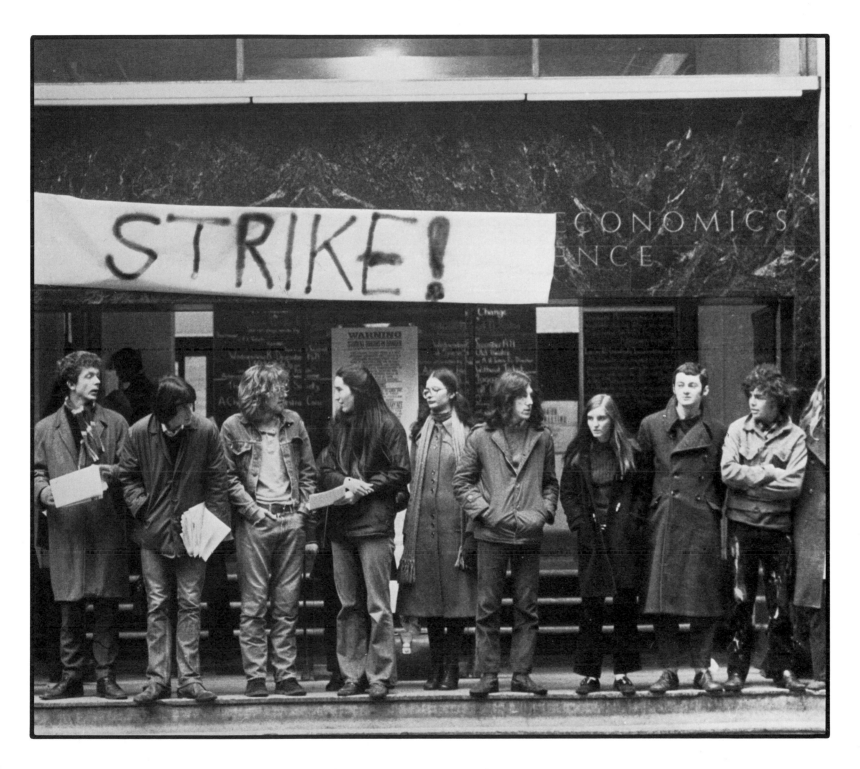

A group of mill girls wait patiently at the front of the crowd hoping to catch a glimpse of King George V who was visiting the town. Oldham, Lancashire. 1913

Women members of the London Metropolitan Police in 1919.

This reveller at the annual August Bank
Holiday Caribbean Carnival in London's
Notting Hill Gate seems to agree that
London's policemen are wonderful. 1978

149

This reluctant swan was found in Palmers Green, London. It would not move. The two policemen were unable to get the bird into the van and it was eventually captured in a net. 1949

A study in expressions. Children of a Chelsea dancing
school at a rehearsal for a water-baby ballet in St. John's
Wood, London. June 1949

Gentle persuasion plus a carrot or two works with donkeys
so maybe it will work with George, a sixty-year-old tortoise
at London Zoo.

London sparrows wait patiently in Hyde Park to receive food from a modern St. Francis. September 1953

A crocodile puts on his best smile for the camera.

Tony, the cat, enjoys a daily walk with his mistress but is careful to keep well clear of the drakes.

156   A cat finds an easy way to catch fish.

Victor the giraffe was grounded in September 1977 and posed quite a problem for his keepers. How do you help a one-ton eighteen-foot high giraffe? Many suggestions, including the use of a crane or the erection of a gantry and winch were received from wellwishers. The story of Victor's problem made press headlines and eventually he was hoisted to his feet with special lifting equipment. The world rejoiced but alas the strain had been too much and Dick, as he was known to the staff at the zoo, died. But the story of Victor was not over as Saturday, June 24, 1978 saw the birth of Victoria, the daughter of Victor's girl friend, Dribbles.

Eton College, the most famous English school, is the home of the Wall Game, played annually between the Collegers and the Oppidans, usually on St. Andrew's Day. The rules state that the purpose is to score a shy or, a rare achievement, a goal.

Robert Fleece's cooper's apprenticeship finished on December 2, 1955 when he was placed in a fifty-four gallon barrel, of his own making. The barrel was loaded with soot, ash, water and other blackening ingredients and rolled around by other coopers in a ceremony dating back to the reign of the first Queen Elizabeth.

The ceremony of celebrating the summer solstice at Stonehenge is an ancient custom practised by Druids, but when the rain came in 1964, Valerie Potter needed protection for herself and her harp with a more modern invention—the umbrella—here held by the oldest Druid, James Duncan.

This young lad on November 2, 1964, was training for an old custom dating back to 1688. Barrels of tar are set alight and the competitor runs through the streets of Ottery St. Mary, Devon. Others pursue and try to take the barrel: the idea is to see who can hold on the longest.

159

OPPOSITE: Pearly kings and queens are peculiar to London and turn out in their buttoned clothing on many occasions, working hard for various charities. The traditional method of transport is horse and cart. A group is seen arriving at the annual Costermonger's parade in 1947.

Helston's famous 'Cornish Floral Dance' has been immortalized in song. Crinolined ladies with their top-hatted escorts danced 'in and out of the houses' and down the beflagged street. 1948

A party of Chelsea Pensioners from the Royal Hospital, founded in 1682, enjoying their annual river cruise to Windsor in 1949. Membership is restricted to Army veterans only.

On special occasions Army personnel are sometimes found carrying odd accessories . . . Lt. Col. Johnston was caught holding the Queen's handbag when she was presenting new colours to the Grenadier Guards in May 1978.

Capt. J. S. McIver, a Padre in the Black Watch was enjoying a cup of tea at Southampton before embarking for Cyprus. He was asked 'Why the umbrella?' and replied 'Just habit!' 1958

'Why do you need a broom?' someone asked Private Simpson of the Black Watch, after his battalion had de-trained at Southampton en route for Cyprus. 'I was the last man off the train and had to sweep up!' 1958

Morris men dance in Tower Hill Gardens.
July 1963

Swan upping is an ancient ceremony per-
formed on the River Thames, when boatmen
representing The Queen, and the Dyers and
Vintners Companies make identification
notches on the beaks of all unmarked swans.
Mr. R. Turk with a feather in his cap was the
Swan Master for the Vintners Company. 1953

The Olney pancake race in Buckinghamshire is a five-hundred-year-old event and takes place on Shrove Tuesday. The competitors of 1949 are shown placing their frying pans at the foot of the church font after the race.

The ancient curse of Lady Mabel Titchborne was again averted in 1947 when tenants of the Titchborne Estate, Hampshire, received their Lady Day dole of flour, in accordance with the eight hundred year old legend. Sir Antony Titchborne was assisted by his six-year-old daughter.

In the years between the two great world wars, the two
minute silence of Armistice Day was strictly observed.
Mansion House, City of London, November 11, 1930.

'Aladdin's Cave' was the nickname given to Piccadilly
Underground Station during the 1939–45 war where
national art treasures were stored in safety eighty feet below
the ground. Travellers on the escalator in 1946 were
unaware of the valuable paintings being carried by
workmen to be rehung in the galleries.

The Emir Ghazi, Crown Prince of Iraq and only son of King Feisal with his latest purchase, a 30/98 Vauxhall Sports. April 1926

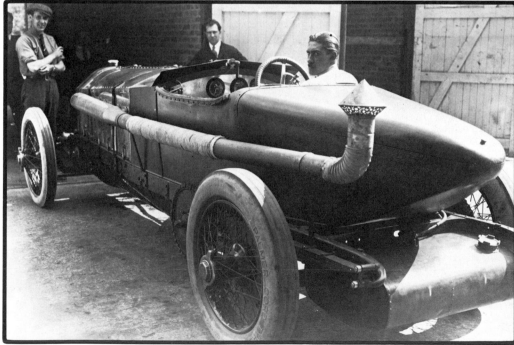

Count Zborowski's Zeppelin-engined racing car 'Chitty Bang Bang'. The car had just been streamlined and a new exhaust system fitted. May 1921

A drive in the park for Lady Warrender and
her friend, Miss Audrey James. April 1921

Royal Princes Albert (foreground), later King George VI, and Henry, later Duke of Gloucester, with their motorcycles which they used for transport to lectures while students at Cambridge University. February 1920

A tunnel beneath the English Channel linking England and France has been discussed for over a century. The start of digging the tunnel at Dover in 1880 is shown in the picture but eventually the scheme foundered.

Trains *can* run on time as shown by this indicator board at Euston Station, London.
June 1946

This scene of London's Cheapside in 1919
shows a wide variety of vehicles including a
hansom cab, and horse-drawn and motor-
buses.

Sixty years later, vastly changed but obviously
the same thoroughfare, Cheapside is still
dominated by the spire of St. Mary-le-Bow
Church—of cockney 'Bow Bells' fame.

Enthusiasts attending a 1947 Herne Hill cycling track meeting had problems recognizing and rescuing their machines after the event.

The Chapman sisters of Kilby, Leicestershire at work in 1953.

The workmen repairing this roadway in 1950 were not prepared to await the return of the car owner.

There were no attempts to control traffic and pedestrians in
Piccadilly in 1919—but it seemed to work.

The City of London in 1929, the historic centre known as
'the square mile' and for centuries the heart of the nation's
financial and business activities. The Bank of England is
shown (right) with Mansion House (centre), the official
residence of the Lord Mayor of London.

The world's most spectacular air show was the annual RAF pageant at Hendon (1920–37). This scene in 1932 shows a Boulton-Paul biplane about to land, with an early glimpse of the famous inflatable 'Blimp'—a wartime defensive kite balloon.

Suitably prepared for take-off in gum boots and hat—Lord Brabazon of Tara, pioneer aviator and holder of British Pilots Licence No. 1 at the controls of his 1910 aeroplane.

The R101, one of the last British giant airships built, flies over St. Paul's Cathedral in 1929. It crashed, caught fire, and was lost near Beauvais, France on an inaugural flight to India in 1930.

179

Polar exploration has always been hazardous.
In 1916 Shackleton lost his ship *The En-*
durance, crushed between the ice floes.

Moving a giant oil production platform is a dangerous task. *Mobil Beryl A* needed five tugs to carry out the tow from a fjord at Stavanger, Norway, to the Beryl Field ninety-five miles south-east of Shetland in the North Sea. July 1975

During the 1939–45 war the giant Cunard liner *Queen Elizabeth* was used as a troop ship and travelled the world. On March 30, 1946, she left Southampton for the Scottish Clyde for reconversion to a luxury passenger-liner.

Derby Day 1910. Behind the scenes at this famous horse race are side-shows, palmists, tipsters and punters on Epsom Heath.

The straight one and a half miles of the Thames 'Henley Royal Regatta' course, was used on this occasion for the 1908 Olympic Games rowing events.

A grand patriotic display by this bookmaker typified the
enthusiastic national feeling at the 1953 Coronation Year
Derby, attended by The Queen and other members of the
Royal Family. The race was won by Pinza, ridden by
champion jockey, Gordon Richards.

OPPOSITE: The Tango demonstrated at an
elegant tea-dance in a London dancing salon.
1914

'Kitty', a well-known flower girl in 1920, at
the south coast resort of Eastbourne, proudly
displays a metal plaque testifying to the
patronage of the town's frequent Royal
visitors.

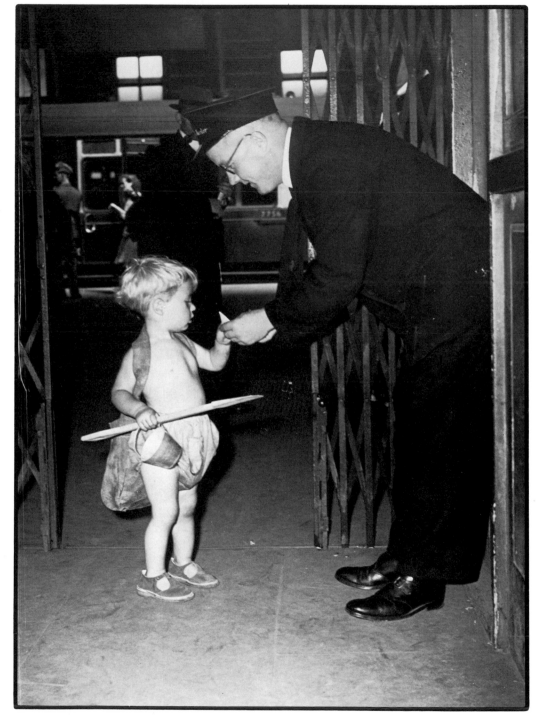

August Bank Holiday of 1947 saw the usual crowds flocking to the railway stations for the seaside. This child was already prepared for the beach.

Two Cockneys from London's Bethnal Green shed inhibitions and take to the national pastime of paddling in the sea while on holiday at Bournemouth in 1948.

A classic seaside pose for the family album
taken in 1914—or did the beach photographer
slowly sink into the sand under the weight of
his equipment?

A cliff-top scene of people relaxing on their annual seaside
holiday at Folkestone in 1908.

This 1908 beach scene at Margate shows holiday-makers well protected from the sun—but fascinated by building sandcastles. Margate Pier, used by millions for day boat excursions to France was destroyed by storms in 1978.

OVERLEAF: Nostalgic songs have been written about London's lamp-lighters and fogs. Thankfully, the 'pea-soupers' have long disappeared, but unfortunately so has the lamp-lighter who used to perform his dusk-duty of lighting those magic, mellow gas-lights. New Year's Eve 1945